Barbara —

[signature]

Barbara —

Dick Martin

I Never Knew the Knife Man's Name

A nostalgic and humorous look back at the days and hours now long gone, but the seconds and moments that linger forever

By

Rona Mann

authorHOUSE™

1663 LIBERTY DRIVE, SUITE 200
BLOOMINGTON, INDIANA 47403
(800) 839-8640
WWW.AUTHORHOUSE.COM

First published by AuthorHouse 11/18/04

ISBN: 1-4208-1204-1 (sc)

Library of Congress Control Number: 2004098893

Printed in the United States of America
Bloomington, Indiana

This book is printed on acid-free paper.

Dedication Page

This book is dedicated to unforgettable memories of hot, sticky nights on a screened-in porch in West Orange, New Jersey. There I would watch endless Yankee games with parents who loved me to the depth of their souls... who would have been so proud that I still remember the brightly colored aluminum glasses from which we drank Hawaiian Punch, the ugly black and yellow fruit bowl filled with apricots, nectarines, and grapes, and damn near everything they ever taught me, whether punctuated with a hug or a spank.

And it is dedicated to all the wacky, wonderful, and loyal friends encountered throughout the various chapters of my life who have in some part contributed to the person I was then, the one I am now, and the one I have yet to become. For a slightly lonely, chubby, wistful "only child" these people became my extended family, with all the joys and annoyances and warts a real family packs in its crazy-quilt baggage.

And finally, and most important, this book is dedicated to Dave, the man who gives me a reason to get up every morning. He has taught me all about Artie Shaw and World War II and how to eat a lobster, and how to perfectly set a watch, and how much life can hurt and love can heal. His will always be the music that makes me dance.

All of these people will forever be a part of me...so therefore, this book must, of course, be part of them.

Table of Contents

What's It All About, Anyway?

This book is not autobiographical, but it *is* about life well lived.

It's about a time of riding a Schwinn bike up and down the sidewalks because you weren't allowed to ride in the street. And about stopping the bike by pushing on the pedals in opposite directions, not by using some silly brake on the steering bar.

It's about so wanting to have a pair of roller skates and then getting a pair that strapped onto your shoes and only being allowed to wear one at a time because your mother was afraid you'd fall down. And of course wearing only one, you did fall, so your parents took them away.

It's about "dressing up" to go to school, church, synagogue, the movies, or just for a trip downtown shopping.

And about saying "Please" and "Thank You" for everything you ever wanted or got.

It's about having to develop and use your imagination because there were no VCRs or DVDs or Game Boys; and learning how to look up information in a dictionary or encyclopedia or a library because there were no computers.

And getting the encyclopedia only a little bit at a time, as your mother went to the supermarket and bought each volume one week at a time if there was grocery money left over.

Or maybe you were rich and a man came to your door fully dressed in a suit and a hat selling the whole set of encyclopedias and your parents would invite him in for Maxwell House and cookies and allow him to go on for hours about how buying the deluxe set would absolutely, positively insure their child's future.

It's about making separate trips to the shoe store and the drug store and the stationery store and the department store because there were no malls...and always knowing the names of all the clerks who also knew yours.

It's about a time when if you bought something, you not only got personal attention, but free gift wrapping...when businessmen bought real estate with nothing more than a handshake, and when absolutely no one made jokes about lawyers or doctors because they were respected for the work they did and their honored place in the community..

It's about a time when the bank was rock solid, the policeman *was* your friend, and your minister, priest, or rabbi was the most trusted individual in your world.

A time when school children were just a little afraid of their teacher, and looked at him or her with complete and utter awe and respect. When if you saw a story in the newspaper it *was* true, because it *was* in the newspaper.

A time when most people dated, got married, and had children... in that order...and those children got spanked if they talked back to their parents.

It was not a time without trouble or hardship, because trouble and hardship have always been a part of time... but it was a simpler time, a gentler time, a time of appreciating more fully, of listening more intently, of loving more unconditionally, and of just being happy *being*.

It was my time.

I Never Knew The Knife Man's Name

I never knew the knife man's name. I don't think anyone did. He was simply, "The Knife Man," and when you heard the unmistakeable clang of the bell as his truck rounded the corner, you knew you only had a few seconds to gather up your dull-edged knives and scissors and run out to the street to flag him down. But know his name? Why? You certainly weren't going to write him a check.

People didn't write checks very much back then, and certainly not for simple services. Today I write checks for everything... manicures, haircuts, teeth cleaning, even to the paper boy. But no, the knife man wouldn't have accepted checks. That wasn't part of his world. His world dealt strictly in metal...gleaming knives and scissors and handfuls of coin as payment.

The knife man wasn't the only man who came to our home back in those sweet, simple days of the 1950s. There was the man who delivered the dry cleaning in paper bags, every Thursday morning at eleven. So regular was his timing, that when I was home from school with the measles or a cold, I knew that at the end of "Beat the Clock" I'd *just* have time to say a quick "hi" to the dry cleaner man before "Truth or Consequences" started. And the great thing was, he always had time to say "hi" back to me and wish me a speedy recovery.

And then, there was "Al the Butcher." I never thought any of these people had last names, I guess, because I never heard any. They just weren't necessary. "Al the Butcher" was really all one needed...it told you what to call him and what he did for a living. Simple. People would be hard pressed to do that now:

Tracey, the Human Resource Specialist?

Jason, the Advertising & Networking Facilitator for the Labor Relations Industry?

Melissa, the Youth Deportment Conservator? (aka babysitter)

Tell me why someone has to be a sanitation engineer today, when years ago "janitor" was a perfectly acceptable term? I think it's all about pride. No one has pride in what they do anymore, so they invent titles to make themselves seem more important. Well, it doesn't matter what you call him, but if the guy takes pride in keeping a clean environment, showing up on time, taking a little initiative in knowing what has to be done to do the job properly, and being friendly to everyone, then there's a damned fine janitor... and what's wrong with that?

Al the Butcher had that kind of commitment to his profession. Each Monday morning my mother would recite her litany into the telephone..." Two pounds of chuck round, four rib lamb chops, some nice chicken thighs (you didn't need to qualify it, Al knew what *nice* chicken thighs were); and by one o' clock that afternoon Al was delivering the order to our door *himself,* each piece of meat carefully and individually wrapped in plain paper, labeled with black crayon. Of course there were no labels indicating fat, sodium, and cholesterol content, because in the 1950s fat, sodium, and cholesterol hadn't been invented yet. And apparently what we didn't know didn't hurt us. We were happy.

Christmas was a wonderful time of year because it meant a great increase in mail delivery, and I never have gotten over the joy of getting mail...of not knowing what pleasure the bulging envelopes or packages or magazines might bring me. As Christmas drew near, we got our deliveries morning and night...best of all, the entire month of December we even had a Sunday delivery...heaven!

One of my favorite delivery people was a character known as "LouietheGarbageman." That's precisely how you said his name...all together as though it were one single word. There really was no other way to do it. We had our garbage can permanently installed in the ground in the backyard. To open the receptacle you had only to tap the lever with your foot, then deposit your bag into the hole and let it slam shut. It was simple, clean, and eliminated odor problems, dogs ripping the bags open, and big messy cans in the kitchen. LouietheGarbageman came on Monday and Thursday to empty the can and tell the latest gossip on his route; and always he peppered his diatribe with a "few clean jokes alright for you ladies."

In addition to his one piece blue uniform, Louie always wore a smile. He never complained about weather, being underpaid, or union woes. He obviously enjoyed his work, his title, and the distinction of being LouietheGarbageman to our neighborhood.

Fred the Milkman always looked like a milkman right out of central casting. His persona and his uniform were as clean and white to me as the milk he carried in the glass bottles... the same milk that if you pulled off the cardboard cap, had a thick covering of real cream on top, just waiting to be licked. If my mother wanted fresh eggs, sour cream, butter, or even ice cream, just a note in the little grey wooden milk box would insure a tip of the cap, a smiling, "Yes, ma'am," and a trip back out to the truck with absolutely *no* complaint.

I was sick a lot as a child...whooping cough, measles, mumps, chicken pox, and literally hundreds of colds and flus...only then the flu was know as "the grippe." No one knows that word today, but when you think of it, grippe was the *perfect* word. That damned virus really gripped you...head to toe, and every place in between!

And when it did, Dr. Baime the pediatrician always came to our house. He wouldn't think of having a child sick with fever bundle up against the winter chill to log time in his waiting room, thereby infecting others. And when a prescription was needed, a call to the local drugstore brought the big blue and tan station wagon up the hill to our home carrying awful tasting liquid concoctions that would cure you quick, but make you beg for ice cream "to get rid of the taste." And for all of this, my mother paid the druggist's bill at the end of the month and slipped some cash into Dr. Baime's hand, and that was that.

But we're MODERN now, and 3 of the scariest letters in our alphabet are H-M-O! The old ways are gone. That old wooden milk box is now painted with flowers and sold at outrageous prices in Vermont boutiques as a keepsake. We have convenient walk-in fast food type medical care facilities for cold and flu. Flu has hundreds of designer names for each strain, and it's all paid for by an HMO that demands you sit in a waiting room for hours picking up other people's germs while exchanging yours. Next you're rushed through an examining room and maybe only see a physician's assistant, they fight with you about paying for a test the doctor recommends, and you stand in long lines at the pharmacy to pay an outrageous co-pay for a medication that's been advertised on TV so much it now commands a fortune. And *then* the HMO raises your premium! And your co-pay. And to top it all off, they tell you the medication is no longer on their formulary list so, sorry, but it's no longer covered!

We're so modern now you don't even have to flush a toilet anymore...know what I mean? In airports, highway rest stops, newer hotels, casinos, and other venues they've taken even that simple task away from you. Now you *"go,"* and then when you look around behind you, which in itself is no mean feat unless you're an Olympic gymnast...where's the handle to flush? Silly, silly you... there's no handle any more. Handles are old-fashioned. You've got to get up first because this damned thing is motion sensitized, and you've got to go into your dance! Except...not all of them respond that quickly. So you stand there like an idiot waving your hands and other body parts around because you've got to get it to flush before you open the stall door! And when you do, the toilet seat takes on a life of its own and starts going round and round like a merry-go-round powered by the sanitized cover machine.

But it's not over...not by a long shot! They don't stop there with all this modern stuff...they've got us again at the sink. You walk over, you want to wash your hands, and...where are the faucets? Where do you turn it on? There *are* no faucets to turn anymore...you've got to motion activate these little babies too!

15

And when you finally do, doesn't the water always stop when your hands have the most soap on them? And then you can't get it to start again. So you have to move to another sink and start all over.

Automatic hand dryers have been around since I was a little girl, but they never stay on long enough. They stop, and you're still soaking wet, rubbing your hands together like Lady Macbeth doing her sleepwalking thing. Please, if the bathroom engineers are out there...if you're listening...will you *please* let us regulate our own bodily functions?

Sadly we don't really need LouietheGarbageman any longer. We have trash compactors. The pure white milkman in his starched uniform is obsolete because we have dairy stores that sell everything from milk to discount books and unfinished furniture. Dry cleaning delivered to the home? It's over... a product of the advent of a whole legion of dry cleaning stores with "in-by-nine-out-by-five service, one hour martinizing, and bring- in- five- shirts- get- one- free promotions. And who needs Al the Butcher when you have mega-supercenters that cover the meat in plastic and label calorie content, fat content, USDA approvals, and cholesterol numbers. Except after all that, you know what? It just doesn't taste as good as it used to!

But...life is better, they say. Easier. Filled with the finest and most up to date conveniences. More modern.

Maybe. Maybe.

But every time I look at a dull knife in the drawer, I still cock my head expectantly as if to hear just one more time in the distance, the sweet clanging of a solitary bell.

I Used to Love Food

I used to love food! Remember food? They don't have it anymore... at least not the food I remember from years gone by.

Take coffee for example. Back when I was a kid every problem in the world seemed to be able to be solved over a cup of coffee.

When people came to visit, my parents didn't entertain in the living room...and who had a family room? Who even *knew* from a family room? The "entertainment center" of the 1950s, and really the center of everything in the house was the kitchen, around the formica table, over a simple pot of coffee. Matter of fact we NEVER entertained in the living room or went in the living room ourselves. The living room was sort of off-limits. It was like a museum...everything in it seemed preserved, and no one could eat or smoke or even sit in there! It was for "best," but "best" rarely happened.

You watched TV in the den, you had coffee in the kitchen, you ate nearly every meal in that same kitchen, holiday meals were served in the dining room, you played with friends in your room or downstairs in the semi-finished basement, but... never, never did you go in that sanctuary with the plastic covered furniture known as "the living room."

Sadly, the time I *do* remember using the living room was when my father died and people came to pay condolence calls. There were so many people that my mother had no choice but to open the living room. In my childlike wonder it confused me that the "living room" was now being used because of death. I guessed that maybe that was what was meant by saving it for "best."

But when I think of the smell of coffee, I automatically think of our kitchen. Coffee in the 50s *was* coffee...real coffee like Maxwell House. Like Peggy Wood served on "I Remember Mama." And if you didn't have time to make a pot of coffee you had instant coffee, and you boiled the water in the kettle and carefully measured out the coffee, and maybe added sugar or milk or cream, and that was that. Simple.

You know that kind of coffee is just about *obsolete* today? Today when you go to a coffee emporium you don't just *ask* for coffee, you have to *choose* from among flavored coffees, cappuccino, latte, mocha, chai, cafe au lait, frappucino, or espresso with steamed milk, a dollop of foam, chocolate and whipped cream...*they* call it "Cafe Mocha"...I call it an ice cream soda! If you want a cup of coffee, do yourself a favor...

have a *real* cup of coffee.

And how about water? Remember water? That obsolete liquid from the "olden days?" You turned on a tap and got plain old H2O. But today you've got herbal extract waters, flavored waters, fiber enhanced, vitamin enhanced, nutraceutical water... c'mon just give me a glass of water! Remember how you asked for it when you were stalling and didn't want to go to bed? "Daddy, can I have a glass of water?" I drank it, you drank it, bad as it was... uninfused and unflavored as it might have been...and guess what? We're still moving around vertically on the right side of the grass!

Then, my friends, there's food. Remember when you ate spaghetti? No one eats spaghetti anymore. We eat *pasta*, and it comes in a lot more shapes and sizes, has a lot of fancy sauces accompanying it, and costs alot more money! When they called it "spaghetti" it was a cheap food you served your family or ate in a diner. Now they call it "Pasta" and people make reservations to eat it in a gourmet restaurant and pay an enormous price for this privilege. *Does this make any sense?*

Remember Yankee pot roast? How often do you see that on the menu anymore? Or chopped sirloin? Liver and onions? Salisbury steak? Peach halves with cottage cheese. Or just plain roast chicken?

But to read a menu today, you need a degree to figure out what kind of food they're serving and how they're serving it:

"Albacore tuna mixed with a caramelized onion, roasted fennel seeds, and dill mayonnaise over mixed greens with a sherry-shallot vinaigrette on Tuscan style panini." Know what that is? A tuna fish sandwich! The difference between what we remember and what you just read is about $6 dollars.

23

Here's another one: Pasta Bolognese. "Sauce prepared with a ragout of veal, beef, and prosciutto, stewed with cheese, cream, garlic, onions, wine, and tomatoes. Topped With Ricotta Salata...$14.50!" Call it what you will, to me it's still spaghetti and sauce!

Or how about this? "A paper thin shell wrapped around a bouquet of diced vegetables, free range chicken, and pork loin, lightly fried in a Thai peanut oil." $6. for two. Do you KNOW what that is? An egg roll! Get it at your local Chinese takeout for 90 cents! *Does this Make Any Sense?*

Ah, but when it comes to desserts we've really lost our minds. Go to New York City these days and the prices of desserts in medium priced to upper scale restaurants are all in the double digits...$12. a dessert and up!

I recently read a specialty dessert menu, and I couldn't understand it! How secure does that make me feel? At a well-known New York bistro they serve a mini chocolate stove over a chocolate coffee opera cake. I have no idea what that is, but they're getting $14. a clip for it!

Or how about "Ravioli of Pineapple and mango with white ice cream?" I thought ravioli had meat or cheese in it...and white ice cream was always vanilla, wasn't it? Have we gotten so taken in by all this that we can't say "vanilla" anymore?

And lastly here's my favorite from another upscale restaurant dessert menu: "Semolina and dried Fall Fruit Tain with Prune-Armagnac Ice Cream and Pan Roasted Apples with Sweet and Sour Cider Caramel..$17.....what the hell is it? I think what it really is, is a fast $17. for the restaurant that's serving it!

I remember a time when food was simply prepared, but enjoyed all the more because you really *tasted* the flavor of that food. It wasn't buried with pretentious sauces and wine reductions. It was cooked to order and was fresh and unassuming and good. It came with mashed potatoes that, and here's a big surprise, didn't have anything in them except real potatoes, milk, and butter. Tell me why every menu today has to have garlic mashed potatoes? Or onion? Or cheddar? Why are we covering up the taste of such a delicious and satisfying vegetable? Does anyone even *remember* what a real potato tastes like?

And salads? Today it's difficult to find just a plain iceberg lettuce salad so preoccupied are we with mesclun greens, radicchio, endive, gorgonzola, goat cheese, and a variety of exotic dressings. A chef may tell you these are complementing the salad...but I pose this question: when you've ladled on the garlic or the gorgonzola, how are you going to taste the simple flavor of the original vegetables?

So I'm finicky and even a bit cranky about my food...I know that. But to me the great chefs of long ago were just simple people like my mother and maybe yours, who shopped a couple of times a week, bought fresh simple foods, prepared them without flash frying them or zapping them in a microwave and brought good honest food that we could recognize to our tables. When you gave thanks at our table for the food, you really meant it...and there was a special blessing added for the cook as well. And if the dessert were finished with anything, it meant it had a dollop of Dream Whip on top. If a sauce had been *reduced*, it meant it stayed on the stovetop too long and there was less of it. And *Hungry Jack* was my uncle approaching the dinner table, not a box of fake mashed potatoes. *Fast food* meant opening a can of Campbell's soup and heating it on the gas stove, and *take out food* could only mean Chinese food. And Chinese food was only Cantonese and meant spare ribs, egg rolls, and wonton soup.

Looking back I sometimes think "potluck" was the best food of all. It meant you had a pot to cook in, you had something to put in that pot, you had a means to heat the pot, and you were fortunate enough to share it with people who appreciated the meal and the fact they could share it together.

Say grace.

The Richest Little Girl in the World

When I was about 4 years old we lived on the seventh floor of a high rise apartment building located at 32 South Munn Avenue in East Orange, New Jersey.

In the basement of that apartment building were a whole series of vending machines...candy...soda...cigarettes...all tantalizing to a 4 year old because of their gleaming chrome and mirrored facades, and the promise of "buried treasure" deep inside. So it followed that one of the highlights of my life came from the great joy I would experience when my father allowed me to accompany him in the elevator for the trip down to the basement to get a pack of cigarettes. He would put a quarter in that magical slot and wait patiently for the sound of the coin falling into the bowels of the machine. Then he'd pull on the chrome handle, the Lucky Strikes or Chesterfields would drop into the bottom tier of the machine, and that's when I would spy my treasure. For in the bottom of the cigarette pack, under the cellophane wrapping were two pennies...change. Change! Cigarettes were only 23 cents a pack if you purchased them from a machine in 1950, and the best thing about those pennies is that they were always new, shiny coins. And they were always given to me! My father would open the cellophane meticulously, handing me the pennies to be deposited in the yellow and red plastic piggy bank I had won at Olympic Park, the local amusement center. To a very impressionable 4 year old those pennies always seemed to be all the money in the world. And holding them tightly in my little fist made me feel rich and special and completely loved by this man I so revered.

Daddy *was* special. I even had a special name for him..."Trusy" (pronounced "troo-zee"), because I told him when I was barely old enough to form the words that he was good and true. And he was! A simple man born in Warsaw, Poland, he had come to the United States when still a teenager. He worked by day and studied English as a second language at night. He met and married my mother and devoted his life to making her happy and secure. He started his own business and worked at it 7 days a week, taking me with him "on the road" on Sunday mornings so my mother could sleep a little later. My father was a master at "customer service" because he valued all people, regardless of what they had or didn't have in life. He visited them at their homes, pet their dogs, gave Charms candies and Chiclets gum to their kids, and always had time to just sit at their kitchen tables and truly *listen* to them. And when we were done seeing everyone he thought should be seen and taken care of, he would let me finish whatever Charms or Chiclets he had left in his pockets, telling me, "Those other ones were for business, but I saved the good flavors for you."

Looking back on those days and our simple, yet special times together, it was those pennies, those pocket candies, and the time my father gave me that made me, without a doubt, the richest little girl in the world.

Uniformity

Something's not quite right.

Remember years ago when you went to a gas station? To begin with, there was no such thing as self-serve. Every gas station was full-serve, and that meant an attendant wearing not only a uniform, but a smile. You were greeted warmly, your oil was checked, the windshield was washed, and maybe you even got S & H Green Stamps merely for making your purchase. And the only time you were the least bit disgruntled was when gas went over 30 cents a gallon.

Fast forward to today!

Gasoline is six or seven times the price, and you get NOTHING! Nobody cares about the level of your dipstick, you pump your own gas at the majority of stations regardless of how you're dressed or what kind of weather it is, and no one even knows what a Green Stamp is anymore. Want your windshield bug-free? Well, do it yourself, buddy. If you're lucky, you might hit a station that has a small bucket of water and a windshield washer wand, but the water isn't changed very often, and the wand is frequently nothing more than a stick with broken rubber. And how do you distinguish who the attendant is? There's no uniform. There's no greeting. No line of chorus boys in starched white outfits is singing, "We are the men of Texaco, we work from Maine to Mexico..." No, your guy is probably the young man on the cell phone. Yeah, that's him over there with the stud in his eye brow, the Mohawk hairdo, and the terse reply when asked for directions, "I have like no idea. I don't like live around here, dude."

Why should I be surprised that the gas station attendants no longer wear uniforms when the doctors don't either? Yesterday's doctor was a professional in a suit or dress with a white coat over the ensemble. Today's doctor wears jeans, boots, and anything from a scrub shirt *you* can buy in the discount store to a tee shirt or tie-dyed affair. Where's the stethoscope? That used to be a dead giveaway of which guy in a crowd was the doctor. Today's doctor often wears an earring...and isn't even a female!

Waiters and waitresses used to look so good! Whether it was a diner and the waitress wore a blue dress with turned up white cuffs at her biceps and a Betty Crocker ruffled apron, or a fine dining restaurant where every waiter wore a tuxedo, had spit and polish shoes, and an expression of caring, the wait staff used to look good. Today there are still uniforms, alright, but in the mass media restaurants they are usually chinos and golf shirts with everything from the restaurant's logo to "Need

Beer?" or "Our Oysters Really Suck!" And the attitude of that wait staff is priceless. Let me set the scenario for you:

You enter the restaurant with your three friends and the host whom you *will* recognize as the one who's playing video games with the beepers they give you when there's a wait for tables says, "Four for dinner?" Nah, you just came by to wait for the bus. (Note: this question is from the same manual the help studies that gets the waitperson to say to you when you are sitting with a dish totally devoid of any crumb of food, "Are you through?" Nah, thought I'd lick the plate first.)

And I have actually been in a fine dining restaurant where the 19 year old tuxedoed maitre d' asked, "Do youse want a boot (sic) or a table?"

So you can see, it's changed.

How many times today have you been in a restaurant where the waiter or waitress greets you with a rehearsed, bored litany of "Hi, welcome to Merlin's Meathouse. I'm Lisa. I'll be your waitress tonight. Do you want to take a few minutes or order now?"

"Well, Lisa, we haven't gotten the menu yet."

"Yeah, right. Wanna know our specials?"

"Actually I believe I'm having a myocardial infarction here."

"Okay then, I'll give you a few minutes. Can I start you with a drink?"

Whether it's the gas station attendant, the doctor, or the waitperson...when the uniform went, so did the personal service. So did caring and respect and wanting to do the job right because it was *your* job to do so.

When I think back I remember the milkman all in white with a cap that got routinely tipped to customers, the postal workers who always wore the colors of the USA with freshly starched shirts and precise ties, and the teachers who dressed for the most important job in the world. And their students who wore dress shirts and trousers, skirts and jumpers, and folded their hands, and paid attention, and listened. And the only time anyone wore sneakers was in the gym. And the crowd outside the church on Sunday morning or the synagogue on Friday night wore the finest clothes they owned. And people said "please" and "thank you" and called each other "Mr." and "Mrs.", and "Yo" was just one part of a child's toy.

But then the 60s came, and we had a "revolution," and we "did our own thing," and somewhere along the line we forgot that the other guy wanted to do his thing too. So we answered it with four letter words and the "me" generation, and a new way of dressing and behaving.

And today here we are... a modern society with too many freedoms and not enough rules, with little respect, and absolutely no regard for the other guy. And we wear what we want when we want and with whom we want. And that's what we teach our kids.

It's still uniformity, but a new kind of uniformity. They call it part of the natural evolution of society.

Personally I think Darwin would cry.

Strubbes

In my town it was called Strubbes. In yours it might have been Mikes or Wolfs or O'Learys, but it didn't matter what it was called. It's what it *was* that was important, and what it *was* was pure heaven. It was that marvelous sanctuary known as the old-fashioned ice cream parlor. Not a pre-fabricated stand, not a truck driving through the neighborhood playing some infernal song over and over, but a *parlor.*

Just thinking about that wonderful word now I get the shivers... not out of emotion, mind you, but because I remember the cold. Ice cream parlors were always dark and cold back then...that was part of their glorious, delicious mystery and charm.

It all started at the front door of Strubbes. It was a heavy door rimmed in dark wood with a big pane of glass and blinds over the glass to keep out the hot New Jersey summer sun.

It took alot to push that door open, but the rewards were great once you got inside. Strubbes had a tile floor with a precise pattern of black and white diamonds that were always gleaming and spotless. The counter was a mile long, or so it seemed, and all black marble on the top with a beautiful rich looking mahogany base. Behind the counter the soda jerks lined up in a row, and gosh, they were perfect! They wore snow white uniforms with black and white aprons, and every one of them had a freshly starched hat with precise points both front and back. But their uniforms were eclipsed only by their talent in making milk shakes, malteds, floats, sundaes, frappes, and scooping fresh ice cream into giant sugar cones and stainless steel dishes.

That's what I remember so well...all the stainless steel behind the counter. The pumps, the levers, the bins where they kept the fresh ice cream...all gleaming stainless steel. And when one of the Strubbes soda jerks opened one to get out a scoop of ice cream he would practically fall in getting the scoop of ice cream out. I always thought those people had the longest arms in the world, and watching them work so hard to prepare *my* ice cream cone was almost as good as the ice cream itself.

Ultimately the prized scoop was retrieved and placed just-so right atop the sugar cone. It never cracked, it was never off-center. It seemed perfect. And then they added chocolate jimmies (in my part of the country they were called "jimmies;" you might have known them as "sprinkles"), handed it to you across the counter, and now the responsibility was all yours... to keep that cone upright, to keep that fragile ball from slipping off center, to work your tongue just one step ahead of the drips...and that was hard work when you were a kid. That was perhaps one of the first lessons in responsibility...of accepting consequences for actions.

Ice cream in the 1950s didn't involve a lot of choice. There was vanilla. Chocolate. Strawberry. And everyone had their favorite. As the years went on Strubbes added coffee, black cherry, maple walnut, chocolate chip. Maybe a few after that, but really, that was all. That's all an ice cream lover needed... the wonderful, pure taste of the cold ice cream and a favorite flavor. Somewhere along the line we got "fancy," and we forgot what good, pure, simple ice cream was. Now stores advertise "96 flavors of soft-serve" and everyone has those blasted mix-ins. Why does anyone want to put a chopped up candy bar or raw cookie dough in a scoop of ice cream? If you want candy, eat candy. If you like cookie dough, go bake something! But ice cream is a treat to be eaten alone...and respected for the unique pleasure it gives.

The days of the simple ice cream cone and the much anticipated visits to Strubbes may seem long ago now, and keeping an ice cream cone from dripping or breaking may indeed be inconsequential given all the problems of our world, but it was those precious afternoons in Strubbes that prepared me for what was to come, and taught me how to cope. It taught me that sometimes you get your licks in and sometimes you don't. That things don't always fit perfectly in the spaces we create for them. That sometimes the cone may break and the ice cream you worked so hard for and looked forward to splats right on the sidewalk in front of you; and when that happens it's okay to cry, because at that moment your whole world *has* indeed fallen apart. So, yes, it's okay to cry and kick a stone and curse at the world and then realize it's only one small cone on one small day in a whole life filled with flavors and toppings and many more chances to experience them once you learn how to push open the heavy doors and take your licks.

Rona Mann

Long Distance

Try and tell a Gen Xer today that once upon a time in the "olden days" a long distance call was a big deal.

A *really* big deal.

Long distance was, first and foremost, expensive. People didn't have long distance calling plans. People did not routinely make or receive long distance calls; and when they did, it was usually to deliver bad news.

If the phone rang, you picked it up, and an operator said, "I have a long distance call for _____," there was a sharp intake of breath as your mind raced wildly, trying to ponder who had died or what horrible event might have befallen relatives far away.

If you *did* have to make a long distance call, most people waited until Sunday, because Sunday was the day that you could call for the lowest rate. Second choice would be late at night, which only served to reinforce the idea that a phone ringing "after hours" must of course be the worst news possible.

So long distance was not the casual "no big deal" it is today.

But the mothers of the 50s and 60s were smarter than the phone company. They had a way around all this. Somehow they all convened for a secret meeting and got together when no one knew, least of all the telephone company...and that's phone *company*, NOT phone *companies,* because in the 50s and 60s there was only the one telephone company...no competition, no diversification.

So at some undisclosed location at some God-awful hour of the night all the mothers in America got together and invented..."the fake phone call." The foolproof way their children could call home from whatever corner of the country they happened to be, and not have it cost a cent. It was nothing short of brilliant!

The fake phone call worked like this: Little Debbie or Stevie would pick up the pay phone, plunk in their dime, and dial the operator. The first thing that happened was their dime automatically came flying down the chute back to them. The second thing was...they got a live body! Not a recording. Not James Earl Jones. Not a menu. But a live, breathing person who ostensibly worked at a nearby telephone center and was not in Bombay but pretending to be in Niles, Illinois. And that person said, "Operator, may I help you?" And they meant it! They wanted to, and more importantly, *could* help you.

But all their sincerity was for naught because Debbie or Stevie was going to fool them... use them shamelessly. This young innocent would say, "I'd like to make a *collect person to person* long distance call to Debbie Schmendrik or Stevie Dinglehoffer at area code 201, 555-2389."

And then the helpful operator would dutifully place the call, Debbie or Stevie's mother would answer...(and note: it was *always* the mother, never the father)...and the operator would say, "I have a person to person collect call for Debbie Schmendrik from Susan Schmendrik, is she there?"

Mom: "No, she's not."

Operator: "When do you think she will be in?"

Mom: "Oh, maybe in an hour."

Debbie: "Fine. I'll call back then after I finish dinner with the little money I have left."

And voila! Message was delivered. Free and to the point.

Mother knew Debbie was safe, was eating, and needed money. What else was new? But moreover, she knew all was status quo in Debbie's world, and that's what mothers needed to hear.

Today we have few pay telephones in public places any longer. They have become the unfortunate victims of a cell phone-obsessed society. People walk or drive down the street with cell phones attached to their heads, playing games on them in doctors' offices, carrying on loud conversations in restaurants and theatres, and sending inane text messages back and forth... because they can.

And the interesting thing about all this is though we *all* have these phones and most of us have unlimited long distance at some time during the week or weekend, and we have the capabilities of doing damned near everything in life on that phone, we are all so busy punching in and text messaging and playing and displaying and diversifying the music on our ring tones, we have completely lost the art of conversation.

Communication has totally broken down. Mother doesn't really know we're safe.

We no longer need face to face interaction with anyone.

We've disconnected.

Sylvia

I guess she was my first real friend. Her name was Sylvia... Sylvia Miles. Later on she married and her last name became Matthews, but it didn't matter much to me because she was always just "Sylvia."

My parents hired her to work for them when we moved from an apartment into our first and only home. Sylvia came several days a week to clean the house and wash and iron the clothes. The latter was her specialty. There was *no one* who could iron a shirt as crisp and perfect as Sylvia. My mother called her "my girl." It was the 50s, and middle class white women who employed Negro cleaning women called them their "girls."...

i.e. "My girl only comes in on Fridays," "My girl was sick last week, and boy our windows need washing." Virtually all of these "girls" *were* black, which makes this prospect seem all the more horrifying in this day and age. It conjures up the very cruelest of prejudice, but back in the 50s it was nothing out of the ordinary; nothing of malice. Young radicals today may recoil when reading this, but that's the way it was. And no one seemed to mind, because in most cases, the "girls" were treated fairly, paid reasonably well, and considered to be members of the families who employed them...invited to the family weddings and bar mitzvahs and first communions. But the fact still remained that most were black, uneducated, and not well off, shoved into a white world as little more than a servant.

I didn't care. I was a somewhat lonely little girl, and my friend Sylvia paid attention to me. Where I was chubby, she was thin and stylish. I thought myself plain looking; Sylvia was pretty. I remember she suffered mysterious headaches sometimes, which I thought very sophisticated and dramatic. When the headaches became too intense to work and Sylvia would call in my mother would say, "My girl is sick and can't come in today." I was an only child, extremely overprotected, and therefore didn't have a lot of friends. I didn't play outside much, because outside was where things could happen to you and you might get hurt. So I played inside.

My world was the cellar because that's where my record player was, that's where my prized Broadway original soundtrack albums were housed, where my toys and games were, and most of all, that's where Sylvia was. While she spent some time upstairs making beds, washing floors, and cleaning the kitchen, she spent most afternoons in the cellar because that's where the washer and dryer and ironing board were located. So when I came home from school each afternoon I hurried downstairs to Sylvia's world ...and mine.

There I would chatter on about school, play a Broadway soundtrack that we had heard so many times the needle skipped over most of the grooves, and I would sing and dance along with the music. And what a great audience Sylvia was for me! She listened intently as she ironed those perfect collars, she applauded my dance steps, she watched me do the same thing again and again without complaint, and she made me feel important when the rest of the world was making me feel chunky and clumsy and unwanted.

If I were sad, she dried my tears. If I had the giggles, she laughed along with me. And when I was sick, she'd come up to my room and chat for a few minutes.

I knew she was different because she was a different color and came from a different world, but I didn't care. In my house she was my friend, and that was all that mattered.

As I got older, Sylvia came less and less because there was less work to do. And then Sylvia's headaches became worse and she would come only once a week. And then not at all.

I was a young teenager listening in on the extension the night Sylvia's oldest sister called to tell my mother that Sylvia had died. My mother wasn't surprised; apparently she had anticipated it. But I felt betrayed because no one ever told me the headaches were *that* bad or that my friend was *that* ill. But I was too angry to cry, so I never shed a tear for my friend Sylvia.

Sylvia's death became the first death of a friend that I experienced, and therefore one of the hardest. I was older now and more aware of the differences between us. She didn't have a fancy funeral, there were few people to mourn her; and a very insensitive woman remarked to my mother, "So you'll get another girl...they're a dime a dozen."

No! Didn't she realize this was *Sylvia*...my first friend, my true friend...a good person who was patient and pretty and had an identity that was defined as an individual, not part of a group all lumped together by blackness and poverty?

And suddenly it was the 60s and our social consciousness was raised and people marched and sang "We Shall Overcome," and Negroes magically turned into "Blacks," and there was Martin Luther King and civil rights for everyone, and murder for some of them, and two water fountains became one, and you could sit anywhere on a bus, and we didn't have to guess who came to dinner. And then the Blacks became "African Americans," and we overcame a little more and pretended that color no longer mattered, and then somehow we got to today.

Not long ago I saw yet another of my beloved Broadway shows. It was called "Caroline, or Change," and in large part dealt with the social changes of the 60s and race and separation and anger.

As the curtain rose, the brilliant performer, Tonya Pinkins who portrayed Caroline a Negro maid, walked down the cellar steps holding her laundry basket. There was Sylvia! Right down to the starched white uniform. But this time instead of a little girl who talked with her and sang Broadway show tunes, there was a little Jewish boy in the play. Somewhat later on in the show the little boy sits on his bed trying to make up with Caroline for an indiscretion on his part. He apologizes by saying, "Let's be friends again!"

The retort from Caroline was swift and sharp. "We weren't *never* friends."

It was then, more than 40 years later, that I shed my first tear for Sylvia.

Hometown

The official certificate bearing the seal of the State of New Jersey authenticates Newark as my official birthplace. But at the time of my birth my parents were living just a few miles west in a suburb called East Orange, so officially East Orange could be documented as my first hometown.

Later on when I was four and the folks had enough money for a home of our own we moved yet another few miles west to a community with the inventive name of West Orange. And it was here that I lived for twelve years, going to grammar school, junior high school, and finally graduating from West Orange High School.

That same summer my mother, now a widow, sold our home and moved to an apartment house in Orange. (You can see a pattern here, can't you? The founding fathers didn't stretch much for names in that part of Jersey). I, of course, moved with her, but only stayed two and a half months, because following the Labor Day weekend I was on my way north to Syracuse, New York to enroll in college.

Initially I didn't like Syracuse. I was homesick, thought it wasn't enough like New Jersey to suit me, too cold, too not-for-me. But somewhere after that first, difficult freshman year I began to really appreciate living in Central New York. So much so that I stayed for nineteen more years! I graduated, got married, owned a business, made wonderful friends, bought a home, then another one, and really made the Syracuse area mine.

In 1983 my husband and I moved to Ohio for a job that didn't work out, but for a while Ohio *was* home. Serendipity brought us back east to Worcester, Massachusetts, Binghamton, New York, and finally a permanent address in Rhode Island.

So...why the recounting of all this geography? Because I have a dilemma. What exactly is my hometown?

Everyone has a hometown...just ask them. It's one of those words that just by its very nature conjures up familiarity and warmth and love and bowls of creamy mashed potatoes, but how is it actually defined? Is your hometown the place you were born, the place you grew up, the place you spent most of your life, or the place you're living right now?

It probably differs from person to person, but to me hometown is where I am today. Where I hang my clothes and where I hang my heart. Where my husband rubs my sore back at night and where I feed the animals. Where we have parties, celebrate birthdays, mourn losses, make friends, and fight silly, insignificant battles.

My hometown is where I can walk or drive down the street and find someone to wave at, where the guy in the post office knows to give me a receipt even before I ask for one, and where I can leave my door unlocked because I want to feel safe in my little world and not afraid of the big one.

My hometown is in the big city and the rural back woods north of the seacoast. It's a place where they have every kind of restaurant and attraction you could want and a place where they roll up the sidewalk at 9PM.

Most of all my hometown is my safe haven, but yet a place that will keep evolving throughout my life as I move from chapter to chapter growing gloriously old with my loved ones, my crazy quilt baggage, and all the hometowns that will forever touch my soul.

Jigsaw

Chutes and Ladders. Candyland. Clue. Jotto. Old Maid. Those were the games of my childhood, the ones my mother would play with me on snow days off from school when the whole world was white and those who knew best thought it was too cold and too snowy and too icy for me to go outside and be a kid.

So I sat inside, bathed in the warmth of my mother's love and more than one cup of hot chocolate with floating marshmallows. And we played together. "Only children" don't have the joy of being pounded on by an older brother or scorned by an older sister or bothered by a younger sibling, so quite often it is a parent who becomes their number one playmate and best friend as well as their primary caregiver.

And on such days my mother would open the closet and get out the games, and we'd wile away the hours together while the snow fell silently outside our window. The biggest challenge my mother had was keeping me occupied, so impatient was I to master something and then move on to something else.

One year for Christmas some relative who must have hated me gave me a child's jigsaw puzzle. I looked it over that disappointing Christmas morning without interest and set the box aside. And there it remained until Hurricane Hazel bore down on us and my mother took the puzzle from the closet shelf, unwrapped the cellophane that still covered the box, and announced, "Come on. This will be fun. Let's put it together."

I stared at those small pieces spread out all over the table and wondered why anyone could ever find this kind of activity fun or challenging. I was uninterested, bored, and very impatient at the prospect of putting this thing together, but my mother remained undeterred. She pushed a few pieces into place herself with great ease and then said, "Now you try."

As she left the room to get the hot chocolate I picked up a piece in my hand. I knew it wasn't the right one and therefore would not fit exactly in the space left to me, but it *was* close. Darn close.

With chubby impatient fingers I pressed it into place, pounding the edges to get a more perfect fit.

My mother entered the room after watching silently for a few minutes in the doorway. "It isn't the correct one," she said quietly.

"But it's close," I protested. "I could make it fit."

"No honey, she argued gently. "If it isn't right...really right...no matter what you ever do, it just will never be a fit."

And then I cried.

Wenches

Remember when you bought something years ago? The advertising that got you in the door was simple, direct, and honest. The people that ran the store were genuinely glad to see you, willing to help you in every way possible, and actually behaved in a manner that made you think *they* wanted to sell you what you wanted to buy.

Bye, bye. Those days are gone. If you want to buy something today, *you* have to do almost all the work...and gee, doesn't that take half the fun out of it?

I mean, let's talk about the advertising. It doesn't matter if you watch the news, a sitcom, or the Super Bowl...do you *understand* half the commercials you see? And then can you honestly tell me that you remember what product it was advertising in the first place? The admen are so busy trying to be funny, cute, inventive, and different that they forget that their original objective was to create a desire in you to actually *buy* some product! And then remember ten seconds after the commercial what product they were advertising!

So now you get in your car or on a bus or a subway and go down to the store, the mall, or the shopping plaza to buy this product and what do you find? Certainly not a salesperson. Not like the ones I remember from my youth. Know what I mean? You go into the store and want help. First of all you have to play that great game called *"Find* the Salesperson." Years ago it was easy. They really stood out. He or she was generally the best-dressed person in the place... impeccably dressed, perfectly groomed, and usually had a professional name tag prominently displayed on his or her clothing. As I said, "Bye Bye! Gone!"

Today if you are in a free-standing mall store it's easier to find the salesperson than in a department store. Just look for the youngest person in the store with perhaps a purple streak in their hair, a pair of faded jeans hanging low on their hips exposing their tummy ring, and no name tag. Why would you *need* a name tag! Just look for the person at the front of the store near the register who's on their cell phone and totally oblivious to the line of customers in front of them! There's your salesperson!

Now, do the unthinkable. Interrupt their phone call by having the audacity to ask a question about their merchandise. You may very well get the universal response of the contemporary salesperson, "I have no clue."

Well, the salesman in Wenches had a clue. He had all the clues because shopping was no mystery back then. Wenches was a popular shoe store in Orange, New Jersey, and *the* place all the moms and dads took their kids before school started each year to get their new "school shoes."

The thing I remember most about Wenches was the big ladder on wheels. My Mom and I would come in, the man in the shirt and tie with the name badge pinned to his shirt pocket would greet us, he would always measure my foot with that cold, weird device that squished your toes, and then he would climb this enormous ladder on wheels and roll up and down the side walls of the place until he had procured several different popular styles in my size. I always sat transfixed watching the salesman at Wenches do that. It looked like a pretty daunting task; and I could never figure out how he could find all those different sizes and then balance all those shoe boxes without dropping a one while he wheeled down the row back to my waiting feet.

That ladder long ago slid down the aisles of Wenches and off into ancient history. Go into a shoe store today...the devices that measure the foot...called the Brannock device, they're still there, but they're shoved under uncomfortable tiny stools, if they even *have* stools. You want to know your size? Measure it yourself, fella! You might have to do it standing up, because there are whole chains of shoe stores now without any place to sit. Need another size? Look for it yourself! Most shoe stores now display all the sizes in stock on the same rack or table. And for those stores who don't display them in this manner, you first have to get the 16 year old *off* the phone, then watch as she rolls her eyes when you ask her to actually *do something* for you.

And then there's my favorite...the stores that tie the two shoes together with plastic because I guess they're afraid you might abscond with the $12.pair of espadrilles. Look, the store has the right to protect itself, but hey, remember the customer? Did you ever attempt to try on *both* shoes and then stand, much less walk, when your ankles are separated by 1 inch of plastic? Give us a break!

Another thing that annoys me today is no one wants to take your money! I may be offbase here, but if *you're* the customer, and you go to a store, and you wheel the wagon around and get shin splints from the concrete floors, and then you stand in line at a checkout, shouldn't there be someone there to ring it all up and God forbid, bag it? Notice how the supermarkets and discount stores and warehouse stores are now all going to what they call "easy self- check out?" The easy part is that the store doesn't have to hire as many people! I just think if I'm dropping money in a particular store it is not unreasonable to ask someone to help me check out! And if you're going to ask *me* to be your checker, then how about giving me a store discount? Or at least pay my health insurance!

Ever buy a large or heavy item and look around for someone to help carry it to your car? Suddenly it's like roaches scattering when someone puts the lights on. There isn't a soul around. And if you are lucky and find someone you might get this for an answer, "It's not my department, but I'll look around and see if I can find someone." And you never see them, or anyone else again, because translated, that answer was," It's not my job, lady. I'm going on my break. And I have a very important cell call to make. Don't bother me. I get off in just two hours so my shift's almost done."

We have the internet now; and while it's a fantastic tool and a wonderful convenience, there are certain things it cannot do. Sure, I can log on to any website in the world and buy any thing.

I can get a great deal at an auction on Ebay. I can go into chat rooms and buy and sell most anything, but with all the search engines at my disposal I just can't find the guy from Wenches. I can buy a wonderful pair of shoes and pay online to have them shipped right to my door overnight; but the shoes will come in a FED EX or UPS truck, not on that magical ladder on wheels. And the guy who brings the shoes will throw the box on the porch, ring the bell, and maybe or maybe not get a signature. Then he's gone. His job's over. He doesn't care if the shoes fit, or if I like them, or if there's a defect in the leather. And he doesn't want to know either. Because that was then. This is now.

And now is some faceless person with their own agenda and a cell phone growing out of their face who's just too busy to know you or care about you.

'Bye, 'bye, Wenches.

When Two Souls Meet

It was very early Monday morning when St. Barnabus Medical Center called. The kind of "early" that makes you jump when the phone rings because it has to be bad news. And it *was* bad news. Mom was dying. She had been dying, in fact, for a very long time, and there had been many calls in the middle of the night resulting in a number of quick trips at breakneck speeds from Syracuse, New York where I was living at the time, down the turnpikes and busy roads to Livingston, New Jersey where St. Barnabus was located. All of those had been false alarms. Mom had rallied and seemed to get better...until the next call and the next hurried trip down the neverending highways. But this morning was different.

79

We had been summoned to New Jersey more than a week ago, and this time we knew enough to stay on. Mom's health was now in rapid decline; and really, it was just a matter of time. So when the phone rang breaking the early morning stillness of June 28, 1971, there was little question that this time was the last time.

The ride to the hospital took only about 20 minutes, but we never made it in time. My mother... my stately, proper, classy, yet hysterically funny mother who rooted for the N.Y. Yankees wearing a fancy robe complete with high heel slippers with an ever- present cigarette in her hand, the woman who had given birth to me when Cesarean section was dangerous, had supported me through every stage of my development, who came to every play, bought all my Girl Scout cookies when no one else would, who dried my adolescent tears, and felt no boy was *ever* good enough to date me... this mother was gone.

I remember that morning so well, right down to what I was wearing, the hard summer rain beating on the hospital roof, and the terrible sound that quiet can make in a room where someone has just died.

So she was gone, and after the shock... and even though death is a certainty, there is *always* shock...and after the tears, come the phone calls...maybe the most difficult part. Those damn requisite calls that have to be made to family and friends even before you begin to think of funeral homes and mourning periods and the settling of affairs.

Cell phones were not a staple of life in 1971, nor had phone cards been invented. I do remember that at the end of my mother's floor were two telephone booths...dinosaurs in today's world. Those large, dark brown enclosures that gave the false impression of privacy, but were in no way soundproof.

And so I began, armed with a handful of dimes, to make those painful calls to our loved ones. With each call more and more tears rolled down my face as the pain of reality grew stronger. This was hell, I thought...and then I heard *him*.

At first his voice burst forth as an intrusion upon my grief. It was loud, boisterous, laughing. I was enraged! My mother was still lying lifeless in a room just down the hall, and this guy in the next phone booth had the nerve to be talking and laughing loudly. And then I heard what he was saying:

"Yeah, ma...it's a boy! 8 lbs. 3 oz...born just after 6AM...he's great! He looks just like grandpa. Naw, she's fine. They're both fine. No name yet, but say mazel tov...there's somebody new in the world!"

Hot tears of anger stung my eyes. How could *he* be so happy when I was so miserable? How could birth be so celebrated when someone on the same floor had died just moments ago? It wasn't fair. It just wasn't fair.

I finished my calls, my hand over my ear to drown out the nauseatingly happy sounds from the next phone booth. And then it was time to leave the hospital and go home to make those most final of arrangements.

The next few days were a teary haze of people coming and going, and food being brought in and sympathy cards, and calling hours, and endless pots of coffee, and... a funeral. And then, suddenly, it was over.

And there it was again...the terrible sound that quiet can make when all the people go away and the true mourning and the reality of living with death begins. A deafening kind of quiet that haunted me day and night.

Yet the one thing I couldn't seem to forget was the man on the

phone in the hospital. Time had brought forgiveness, or should

I say, reality. Of course he had the right to be happy. His wife

had just borne him a son. A boy that came into the world on

June 28, 1971 at just about the same time my mother had died.

And so I started to fixate on that baby. What did they name

him? Was he growing strong? Did he have a lot of hair? Was

he being nursed or bottle fed?

They're right, you know, all those damn people who tell you

"time is a great healer" when you least want to hear it. But

they're right, and without so much as your permission time

grabs life by the tail and powers it forward... thrusts it toward a

future, like it or not...that's the part they don't dare to tell you.

And pretty soon it's the 3rd anniversary of her death, and I'm

spending the day wondering if that little boy is in pre- school.

And at her 5th year anniversary I'm thinking about *his* first day of school. And then in a blink it's 1981...ten years since her death...and his birth, and I'm wondering if he's a N.Y. Yankee fan like she was, or in Little League, or eating the Girl Scout cookies his sister might have had trouble selling.

In 1989 I am thinking again...this time about his high school graduation, perhaps taking place on his birthday, and wondering to myself if he's going on to college, or the service, or a job.

And now that it's more than 30 years since that June 28th I'm so very curious to know what he's done with his life, this now full grown man. Did he marry? Does he have a family? What are his dreams and hopes for the future? I've so often thought of contacting St. Barnabus Medical Center to see if they might give me his name so I could try to find him and ask him these questions myself; but I missed any chance of that a long time ago. Now we have stringent privacy laws, so his birthright and vital statistics are fiercely protected forever.

And maybe that's how it should be. Maybe he was put on earth for a variety of reasons, not the least of which is that his birth touched me, a total stranger...because every June 28th for now and for the rest of my life I will always think of those two souls...one going out, one coming in, perhaps crossing for just a moment somewhere in the universe, each on his own way home.

Crime And Punishment

When I was about nine years old, I committed a crime.

Actually it was a pretty heinous crime for the day.

I came from a good family, I lived in a decent middle class neighborhood, and I was a good girl most of the time. My parents worked hard to teach me the difference between right and wrong; and yes, I got punished when I violated the rules they had set down.

I even got...*spanked!*

Did I shock you? Yes, I got spanked. And more than once, let me tell you. To this day I am one woman who doesn't worry about *any* dessert going to my rear end, because I don't *have* a rear end. Why? Simple. I used to have one, but I also had a smart mouth as a kid, and that didn't fly in my father's house.

But was I abused? Hell no! Battered? Not at all. Matter of fact I can remember my Dad with tears all welled up in his eyes as he had me over his knee, because he didn't really want to spank me at all. But somehow he managed to conquer this little psychological roadblock, and I got walloped. And I'm here to tell you that I didn't call the police to report child abuse, nor have I ever frequented a psychiatrist's couch because of it. I needed it! But today we have evolved. We have no need to be physical because now we have..."time out."

Time out? The only time out my father condoned was the one *he* took just before he whaled on me!

What is this stuff today about "time out?" You send a kid to his room for a period of time and call it punishment or a cooling-off period. Punishment my foot! In that room... in that horrible holding cell...is a TV, a VCR with DVD player, Game Boy, and God-knows-how-many tapes, video games, a computer, and a cell phone. That isn't a time out...that's heaven for the little yard ape!

I have a friend in Connecticut who tells me about "The Attitude Corner." She puts her son in the "Attitude Corner" to think over what he's done, but not to...and this is critical here... "in any way alter his self-esteem." Are you kidding me? In my father's house *he* was the only one allowed to have an attitude, and *I* was the one who got put in the corner. I was just a kid, and in those days it was your parents who ruled the roost and you weren't *allowed* to have self-esteem. You didn't even know what it *was* that you weren't allowed to have!

Self- esteem aside, let us now return to my heinous crime. I grew up in New Jersey where summers were hot and oppressively humid, and the mosquitoes were so big they had leashes.

I never liked summers...probably because it was hot, oppressively humid, and the mosquitoes were so big they had leashes. I can remember night after night lying awake in bed for hours listening to those hated insects intone their monotonous whine above my head, living in fear I would get bitten.

My mother tried valiantly, but unsuccessfully, to help. She bought the mosquito elixir of the day...6-12. Remember 6-12? It was a very, very thick, sticky, sweet smelling oil that came in a clear glass bottle. The idea was to slather the 6-12 all over your body, and according to the advertising on the bottle it would keep the mosquitoes far away. So every night I would grease up as though I were going to swim the English Channel. And 6-12 had the following result: by the time you had covered your arms, legs, and any other exposed body parts, your hand was so greasy that you either dropped the bottle onto the floor, in which case you would have to purchase another bottle, or you couldn't pick up the cap to put it back on the bottle. And in addition to all this, 6-12 did absolutely *nothing*, except for the guy's bank account who invented it. It smelled so sweet that the mosquitoes, attracted to it, now came in swarms... I was their candy store. Their single whiny voices now blended together in chorus, and they bit the living hell out of me. I was a chubby, miserable, greasy little Jersey girl.

So as I lay there night after night all greased up and waiting for the expected onslaught, I would think up things to do to pass the time to take my mind off the imminent mosquito attack. One night while tossing and turning, my hand came upon the tag that hung off my pillow. I remember my mother telling me NEVER, NEVER to remove that tag, but she never said why.

So this night I got my flashlight out and shone it on the tag. It was ominous, because it stated in no uncertain terms that it was against the law to remove that tag. I shuddered in fear wondering what would happen if I just *accidentally* removed the tag. I mean what if I rolled over one night a bit too roughly and it came off...that wouldn't be my fault, right?

Well, my nine year old curiosity finally got the best of me, and one night I made just the tiniest tear in the tag. My heart was pounding, and I sat erect in bed wondering if somehow it was connected to some master board that signaled the manufacturer, and soon they would come in a police car and take me away. But nothing happened that night. Nor the next night when I tore just a little more. Nor the one after that. With each succeeding night I got bolder and bolder until that tag hung from the pillow for dear life by just a single thread.

And therefore the very next night I decided *this* would be the night. Obviously this pillow tag business was the biggest lie ever perpetrated on the American public, and *I,* this little nobody from New Jersey, would be the one to prove it a hoax.

I steadied myself in bed feeling a strange sense of euphoria. I put the pillow in my lap and nonchalantly stroked it, turned it over, and played with it for awhile. I made sure everyone else in the house had gone to bed and all was quiet. Very, very quiet. Then with one deliberate motion from my chubby fingers I pulled the tag free...and at that very moment an ambulance, I guess, or a fire engine, or a police car...whatever it was... came roaring around the corner outside my window with the siren screaming loudly.

I wet my pants.

Recipes Aren't About Food

Recipes aren't about food. They're not about how many cups of flour to add, or what method should be used for creaming together the butter and sugar, or whether you can substitute dried onion flakes for the real thing. Not for one minute. Recipes are about people. About your Grandmother Elizabeth and my Aunt Fanny and someone else's Cousin Lucy.

They're about well worn pots in which they always used to make such and such and so and so, or the special bowl with the crack on the side that Frieda always used when she whipped up her special frosting, or the pink plastic bowl Mom used to put the chicken noodle soup in when I had the grippe. Or the

Thanksgiving platter that no one likes, but it's been in the family for so many years that nobody can remember who originally bought it or gave it to whom as a gift, and yet <u>must</u> be used no matter which house hosts the feast each year.

And recipes are about traditions like always having creamed oysters at Christmas, even if no one likes them. Or having *real* cranberry sauce with orange rind for everyone else, but the jellied kind in the can for Uncle Ralph because it wouldn't be Thanksgiving for him without it slithering onto his plate.

And recipes are about friendly and not-so-friendly familial relations like the time Cousin Beatrice gave Cousin Edna the directions for her Casserole Supreme, but conveniently forgot to include an important ingredient...and to this day, though they haven't spoken in over 10 years, Bea swears she did *not* omit the eggs.

Recipes are about families and traditions and feelings. They're about the tear in your eye when you sip the soup your great-grandmother made, and the gentle smile that comes across your lips when you stir the chocolate into your child's glass of milk the way your mother did when you fell down and skinned your knee.

The recipes of long ago did not have a lot of ingredients. They didn't require you go all over town to find a special gourmet can of some East Indian spice. They were plain and simple, and the food just tasted good. You didn't have to decorate the plate with squiggles or put a sauce all over it or make a pyramid of the food to have your meal be a big hit. If you could make a radish rose, you were a genius!

And best of all, the real old fashioned cooks had their own units of measurement, and they were *nothing* like those they teach in today's fancy cooking schools. Their ingredients were not measured in teaspoons, tablespoons, or cups. The amounts were judged accurate to the mix by a wise eye, a pinch of the fingers, or a freefall of liquid ingredient.

Those recipes of long ago were scribbled on torn pieces of paper that hung out of The Settlement Cookbook or The Joy of Cooking, and got stained and brown at the edges, but were never recopied...or heaven forbid, put on a computer disk.

In one of my recipe boxes carefully filed under the proper headings, and yet never prepared by my hand, are recipes copied in my mother's precise bookkeeper's handwriting...a handwriting cultivated after years of the Palmer Method taught in her grammar school. And each of these recipes has no fancy culinary title, but a nomenclature that tells you exactly what you need to know: *Helen Kadish's Wonderful Apple Kugel, Emmy's Cranberry Mold that She Always Makes for Thanksgiving, Jeanne's "Larry Thinks They're Diet Macaroons."* See what I mean? Nothing, absolutely nothing, was left to the imagination!

I move my fingers slowly over my mother's recipe box. It's dark brown with handpainted chefs, the head of a steer, and the word "Recipes" on the front. It's not terribly attractive. It's worn. The design doesn't even make a lot of sense, but the box perpetually sits on my kitchen counter. It has sat on the counter of every kitchen in every home and every apartment I've ever occupied. Its recipes are safely tucked inside. I never create them and rarely open the box at all. But I know they're there, and they serve as a connection to another time and a beloved woman whose best and worst habits I've managed to inherit even though I swore as a teenager I'd never *ever* do.

Recipes are not about food.

The End

Living a life is a real tough job. It takes up an awful lot of your time, all of your weekends, it cuts into your holidays and time off; and in the end, what do you get out of it? I think actually that the life cycle as we know it is completely backwards. You should die first...get it out of the way. Get it over with! Then you'll go live for 20 years in a home for the aged. You'll play a lot of bingo, eat an awful lot of tapioca, and spend most of your time there reminiscing, no doubt getting some of the names and events and dates mixed up, but it won't matter, because you'll remember how good the old days felt... and that's the important part. Then one glorious day you'll get kicked out of the home because you're too young. Someone will give you a gold watch, and then you'll go to work. You will work at least 40 years at something you hate until you're young enough to enjoy your retirement. And you *will* enjoy your retirement! When you've had enough of that, you'll get accepted to college and you'll happily become a coed again. And boy will you ever party! You'll party until you're ready for high school. And off you'll go to classes and football games and pep rallies, and maybe even become the king or queen of the prom. Next you'll become a little kid again. You'll play. You'll play hard. And one day you'll undoubtedly fall down and skin your knee and cry. And someone will pick you up and hug you and kiss your boo-boo... and somehow everything in the world will be all better. You'll have absolutely no responsibilities at all now. So there's nothing to do but become a little baby again, and coo and drool and explore every corner of your playpen. And then one day you will go back into the womb. You'll spend the last nine months of your life floating blissfully. And you'll

wind up as a twinkle in somebody's eye.

THE BEGINNING

About The Author

Rona Mann started living her memories in New Jersey. She has since lived them in Syracuse, New York; Ohio, Massachusetts, and has been making memories with her husband in Rhode Island since 1986. A graduate of Syracuse University with 2 degrees in Theatre, Rona has performed in summer stock, off-Broadway, in Repertory Theatre, and on Radio. She is a proud Rotarian, writes professionally, and previously published a book "Ghosts Along The Road," an offbeat accounting of the small roads in coastal Rhode Island and Connecticut.

She performs "Knife Man" anywhere there's an audience waiting to reminisce, laugh, cry, and enjoy. She respects the past, loves the present, and waits with great anticipation for the future.

Printed in the United States
72198LV00005B/418-513